# Picking Up the Pieces and Creating a Life I Love

STEPHANIE C. SMALLS

**BALBOA**.PRESS

A DIVISION OF HAY HOUSE

Balboa Press books may be ordered through booksellers or by contacting:

Balboa Press
A Division of Hay House
1663 Liberty Drive
Bloomington, IN 47403
www.balboapress.com
844-682-1282

Because of the dynamic nature of the Internet, any web addresses or links contained in this book may have changed since publication and may no longer be valid. The views expressed in this work are solely those of the author and do not necessarily reflect the views of the publisher, and the publisher hereby disclaims any responsibility for them.

The author of this book does not dispense medical advice or prescribe the use of any technique as a form of treatment for physical, emotional, or medical problems without the advice of a physician, either directly or indirectly. The intent of the author is only to offer information of a general nature to help you in your quest for emotional and spiritual well-being. In the event you use any of the information in this book for yourself, which is your constitutional right, the author and the publisher assume no responsibility for your actions.

Any people depicted in stock imagery provided by Getty Images are models, and such images are being used for illustrative purposes only. Certain stock imagery © Getty Images.

Print information available on the last page.

ISBN: 978-1-9822-7037-7 (sc)
ISBN: 978-1-9822-7039-1 (hc)
ISBN: 978-1-9822-7038-4 (e)

Library of Congress Control Number: 2021912618

Balboa Press rev. date: 07/21/2021

# DEDICATION

To my mother and father – Veronica Smalls and Isaac Smalls – who have given me a life-long supply of love, support and laughter.

To my mentor – Teressa Moore Griffin – who encouraged and believed in me as a writer long before I did.

To everyone else – Love yourself and know that you are enough.

# CONTENTS

# THE "BROKEN" PIECE

## DIVORCE

Our marriage had been in demolition mode for those last few years, until the end was finally imminent. Unhappiness, disappointment, and silence had been consistent guests in our home. I think most people want to hold on to what is familiar, what feels normal and morbidly safe, but when you open your mind and toss around what's best for you, you have to be completely honest with whatever that may look like, even if it means going your separate ways.

As painful as it is, divorce can be a positive thing for both people involved. Big changes, life changes, are extremely challenging, especially the ones that are unplanned, the ones you didn't see coming, or even the ones you saw coming but placed on the denial shelf, safely tucked away to possibly be revisited later. Big changes, life changes, the ones that knock you over, the ones where the pain is so torturous that it feels like it has to end in death, yet somehow you keep having the ability to breathe. When you think something is going to last forever and it doesn't, it can be debilitating. The failure of something, anything that you love and hold dear and lose, can be a crippling experience. I wanted to rescue us; we were supposed to be one of those couples that made it through the hard times so that we could bask in the sunlight together as we grew older. I thought we had what it takes, but sometimes things are destined to fall apart.

After realizing that it was really over, I was consumed with shame, guilt, embarrassment, insecurity, fear,

uncertainty, hurt, and regret. Shame because we broke it and just couldn't fix it. Guilt because I kept wondering if we fought hard enough to save us. Embarrassment because I said "till death do us part" in front of 125 friends and relatives at our wedding. Regret because I lost a family that I loved so dearly. The list goes on and on.

Divorce is extremely painful because it represents the loss of a partnership, the loss of dreams, and the loss of commitments that were once shared between two people. Having to move on and let go of what I knew I should leave in the past while opening myself up to whatever came next was difficult but necessary for my survival. I had so many uncertain moments. Those times when I was OK but not quite there yet. Those times when I knew there was growth but had nothing tangible to show for it. I remember the days when it felt like everything was falling into place, yet I would still go home and cry myself to sleep because the thought of being alone was real and apparent. The thought of

having to get up each morning filled with uncertainty, with nothing on the agenda except getting through the day, was exhausting. What about those days when I took two steps forward and one step backward? Would I ever get ahead?

I didn't know then, as I navigated each step with the intention to move forward, that it was OK to be unsure. I did not yet recognize that growth can be as painful as it is beautiful. The craft of letting go of the old, of not being held hostage while receiving the new, was scary and unknown but still very much learnable. I remember often thinking, *If I can stop beating myself up for a moment, I just might realize how far I have already come, while at the same time knowing and acknowledging how far I have yet to go.* I would get up, make myself look beautiful, go out, and smile despite what my reality was and how I was feeling on the inside. I remember wondering what people would think if they could see the invisible bubble above my head that screamed, "Help me! I can't do this!" Most people wouldn't believe there were

weeks when six out of seven days I didn't feel good enough; I doubted every positive thought that entered my mind. I just didn't trust myself. How could I? My marriage failed and there didn't seem to be anything we could do to save it.

There were so many days when I would sit and cry, reflect, pray, and try to gather strength to get up and keep moving, days when I wondered whether anyone would notice that I was missing if I stayed under the covers for a year. A part of me knew that one day I would discover the lessons that I was supposed to learn through all of the emotional trauma brought on by the dissolution of my marriage.

I would know soon enough that divorce has not destroyed me, that I didn't have to stay shattered, and I always believed that God was able to restore what was broken and change it into something amazing. And even though I was walking on shaky ground most days, I was still able to recognize that one day things would come together and start to resemble

something familiar and beautiful: *me*. But I didn't know then that all the broken pieces would return later in my journey and be put back together in a way that I never could have imagined. As I do the checks and balances of my life, I have to remind myself that I am not a failure. There may be times when I feel like I can get to an amazing place yet still feel like a part of me is missing once I get there, and that's OK. I have learned what it means to mourn and grow simultaneously. I now have a daily mantra of letting go of what I need to leave in the past and moving on to whatever comes next in the future.

# THE "GIRLFRIENDS" PIECE

## LOYALTY AND LACK THEREOF

ne of the hardest things to accept while on this journey has been the changes in friendships. See, I don't have blood sisters; I am the younger sibling of my one and only brother. When you are going through a tough time in your life and are broken, confused, lost, lonely, depressed, and sad, you just want your girlfriends to scoop you up, engulf you in their sisterhood of love, and laugh their asses off with you. It's a time when you should feel not judged but accepted by your sister-friends.

I remember being warned by someone that through the process of divorce, I would see who my true friends really were and learn to believe what I am shown. I shrugged off that comment because not for one moment would I believe that anyone in my sister-friend circle wouldn't be there for me and allow me to rest in their love, trust, and support.

I am sorry to say that I have discovered, during my toughest days throughout this journey, that friendships indeed do change. I found out that some weren't willing to scoop me up during my time of need, and some felt conflicted about supporting me. Some went completely silent. Some felt that I had separated myself, when if this were the case, it was only due to my circumstance; hence, the need for my true girlfriends to come rescue me as I was drifting out to my emotional sea. I tried to stay involved but felt the disconnect growing and learned through the grapevine that events and gatherings were taking place that I once was a part of. I was either purposely being excluded or just not invited to join.

Even though I know we can't all be invited to everything, this broke my heart because I always prided myself on being a true sister-friend and just assumed that I would get the same in return.

I am naturally drawn to strong women and to the connections that we have between us. I believe that we learn so much from each other by spending quality time together and sharing our life experiences while connecting and supporting each other at the same time. The one thing I thought I could always count on was my girlfriends. And even though my feelings were hurt to the core, I knew that I couldn't stand in those feelings for too long; instead, I had to understand that some friendships don't always turn out the way we think they should, and some don't always go back to the way they may have been before. Some were surface friendships and weren't as deep as I once believed they were. I have learned that some girlfriends come into your space for a specific reason, and some just aren't meant to be lifelong.

One-sided friendships have never served me well, and I have finally learned that letting go of those friendships and any negativity or anxiety that came with them is in my best interest and will support me in my growth. I had to stop myself from reminiscing about people who hurt me, learn that not everyone wants me to win, and accept that I may not be everyone's cup of tea. I had to understand and accept that not everyone deserves my vulnerability. I couldn't continue to pour into people who were not willing to pour back into me because doing so would make me feel empty and exhausted. I also learned that friendship intimacy is just as important as relationship intimacy, and both need plenty of care and attention.

After all of those lessons, I now keep my circle very small and only trust and become vulnerable with those who give me the same in return. I had to look closely at the girlfriends who supported me and checked on me regularly for weeks and months on end. I was pleasantly surprised to grow closer

to certain women who were more than happy and willing to scoop me up and include me in many exciting events and activities, inviting me and taking me out so that I could have a good time as I was learning to maneuver in my newly single status. These girlfriends understood that I just needed to get out and have fun and were willing to hold me close as I was trying to find myself again. I entrusted these women with my heart and shared many emotional conversations with them. There would be days when I would randomly receive a floral arrangement or other gifts of love, all to make me feel better in hopes to simply put a smile on my face. I felt love, grace, acceptance, kindness, and reassurance during a time when I was very much shaken and uncertain. Lisa, Yvonne, Ava, Christine, Jamie, Ruth, Ginny, Nikki, Amy, and Monisse, thank you for being there for me and reminding me of my value, strength, perseverance, and confidence.

# THE "HEALING" PIECES

## THERAPY, GROWTH, TRANSFORMATION

am a true believer in therapy and coaching for purposeful, conscious, and intentional healing. I believe in working with someone I trust and connect with to peel back the layers to discover and work through the root of issues that may be so deeply buried that I wasn't even aware that they were there.

For me, therapy is a tool to help set and achieve goals, improve communication skills, and learn where all my emotions are deriving from. I wanted to heal from the

inside out while learning and understanding that the road to personal empowerment is paved with self-reflection, growth, surrender, and transformation and will take a lot of work for me to see the results. There is so much power in self-love, and I wanted to get a better understanding of what I needed to do in order to love myself first and foremost. I knew that it was my responsibility to edit and make the proper changes for myself to achieve the life that I wanted. I also wanted to create a new narrative in my head about who I was. No longer was I going to believe that I was less than what God created me to be. No longer was I going to believe that my ideas were mediocre, for nothing about me is average. I strive to be more grounded within myself. Peace was something that I was pursing on a regular basis, and I knew that trusting and relying on myself emotionally would change my life for the better.

I had several goals, but one of my growth goals consisted of sitting in my silence, being still and present with my

thoughts, finding comfort in being alone, learning what it means to truly have faith, and giving it to God and leaving it with him. A coach of mine once suggested that I purchase a God box: write down my worries, fears, and any specific things that are giving me anxiety on a piece of paper, fold it up, and give it to God by leaving it in the pretty box. Sometimes putting a physical action to a thought process helps you to feel like you are actually doing something to aid in the process of healing. I wanted to worry less and set boundaries for others as well as for myself.

Self-care became my number one priority because I knew that it was something that only I could give myself exactly the way that I needed it. A big aha moment for me was recognizing that change happens whether we accept it or not. Sometimes change knocks us over the head so hard it gives us emotional whiplash. I was open to learning some strategies to be able to withstand challenging times.

Part of being open to change and leaning into it is moving past helplessness and hopelessness while focusing on ourselves and knowing that we deserve the positivity it may bring. My strength and inner fierceness come from nothing but God. It is he who has kept me alive, sane, and grateful while my mother and father are the spine in my back that enables me to stand tall and proud every day.

My mother is my anchor, my best friend, and my soul mate. The friendship that we have is unmatched and unlike any other. Her soul is filled with empathy and compassion, and everything I know about love, I learned from her. Her heart is one in which you can see. She is the kindest and most giving person on the planet and knows every nook and cranny about her daughter.

My father is also my best friend, my leader and advisor, and the true standard of what a man is and should be. He

has Superman qualities and is capable of the impossible. His brilliance is rare, remarkable, and extraordinary.

The love and adoration my parents have for me I will never know from another living soul. They have given me so much love and support that it has fueled my life and keeps me wanting only the best for myself because they taught me that I am worthy of it. They get to watch me move through the world and are proud of the woman I grew to be.

Learning to transform and grow is a wonderful healing process, and what I know for sure is that I am better for it.

# THE "SELF-DISCOVERY" PIECES

## ME, MYSELF, AND I

The journey to self-discovery is not easy. It includes fear, confusion, misunderstanding, and doubt and forces you to revisit all of your choices in your life, especially the bad choices. But it also includes happiness, fulfillment, clarity, and enlightenment. The journey could require making some tough decisions and sticking to them. It includes setting intentions, being more aware, paying attention to your own feelings, and understanding yourself by being true to who you are. It includes recognizing my strengths as well as my weaknesses.

My mother has told me that I am one of the most resilient people she has ever known. I had to do some of my own research to make sure I truly understood the components and what it was that she saw in me. Resilience is having the capacity to recover quickly from difficulties. It's toughness. It's having the ability to cope with stress and adversity. It's having a positive attitude, being full of optimism, and having the ability to regulate emotions.

Through my self-discovery process, I became very self-aware and learned a lot about myself. I learned that I have deep joy that lives inside me. I am so grateful for it because it has allowed me to be confident, keep smiling, stay light, and give off a positive vibe that others find to be pleasant and want to be around. Energy is everything, and I truly believe that what goes out is always going to come back.

I want to always come from a place of compassion and a willingness to understand and be understood. My goal is

to always put out positivity and encouraging dynamics. I believe that we create our own reality; we choose to believe what we want about life. Choose to be happy, and it will be so. I try to create a vision to see the world through the view of happiness, and doing this has shaped my reality. Through my self-discovery process, I have learned that I am the kind of person who is able to totally forgive someone who has hurt me, and I am proud that I have the ability to just focus on the good in them and leave the bad in the past.

Forgiveness is for me and my personal growth and not the person who hurt me. I have a "moving on" mindset that is one of my strengths. I like to address things, get a better understanding of your perspective, share my perspective, either agree or agree to disagree, and move on. I don't want to live looking in the rearview mirror.

Self-discovery can also shed the light on some challenging things that can take considerable time to sift through. I

know that I am a taskmaster and that I have a need to take command of any situation. I am very much a solution-driven person who enjoys being in control. I always feel the need to find the answer and fix it. If something hasn't been tended to, it makes me feel very uncomfortable, as if it has been left undone. I hate for things to be what I call "loose and fussy." It's hard for me to relax unless the problem or issue has been resolved. I recognize that I am detail oriented and like solid solutions. I like to tie things up in a bow and move on to the next thing.

The need to control, manage, and do it myself are probably things that I will always struggle with letting go of, because it's just a part of who I am, but they are also things that I continue to work on to minimize my anxiety. In order to relieve myself of stress, I have to challenge myself periodically and leave certain things as they are.

There were many times throughout this self-discovery phase when I had to ask myself several questions so that I could get to know myself better. The trick to each question was to answer them with total truth and honesty. I asked myself, "Who am I? What do I want to offer the world? What excites me? What makes me happy? What do I need for my own emotional awareness? How do I create a life that I love? Do I feel hopeful? Am I open? What will I accept in my life and in my heart?" I found it helpful to create a list so that I can visually see the attributes that are important to me and make me feel good; that way, I can remind myself of what kinds of characteristics and likenesses I want to surround myself with. Specific types of people, specific places, and specific things.

It's very important to know what you like so that you can seek those things and welcome them into your personal space. Here is a small snapshot of my personal list:

**People:** resourceful, authentic, consistent, kind, giving, loving, affectionate, warm, fun, God-fearing, adventurous, funny, spontaneous, interesting, outgoing, patient, perceptive, loyal, thoughtful, intelligent, inquisitive, honest, attractive, communicative, open-minded, respectful, organized, self-aware, mindful.

**Places:** ambiance, picturesque, trendy, charming, contemporary, cosmopolitan, water, beaches, fascinating, diverse, chic, inclusive, warm, cultured, exciting, popular, bustling.

**Things:** music, spa, champagne, shoes, dancing, fashion, food, writing, décor, cooking, cuddling, walking, hugs, compliments, candles, intimacy, wine, my cozy and comfy bed.

You must know what you want and what you deserve so you can provide yourself with those things. Allowing

yourself to engage in the things that will give you happiness, comfort, and fulfillment are the best way to create a life that you love.

Part of being on the self–discovery path is that the road never ends. There is no finish line. There is always something to learn and discover about myself because I am constantly evolving, and that is very exciting.

# THE "DATING" PIECE

## GREAT MEN!

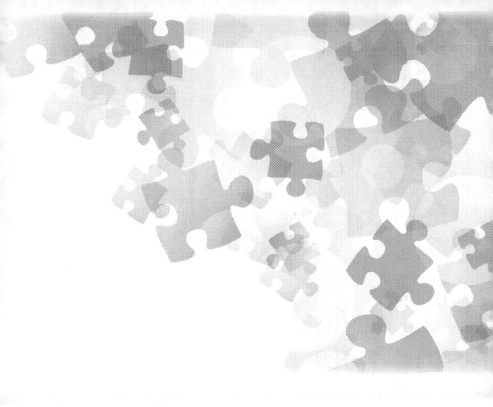

never thought of myself as an expert on dating, but after the year I had of "serial dating," I can honestly say that I learned enough to teach a course!

The first lesson in dating is having confidence and knowing that you are all that you embody and truly believing that it is an honor for any man who gets the opportunity to spend time with you. I knew that I had something special to bring to the table. I confidently believed that I was sexy, classy, interesting, open, smart, and funny. I've been told

that I have a dynamic personality and I knew that it would attract men like a magnet, and that is exactly what happened.

After coming out of a divorce, the last thing that I wanted to do was to jump into another relationship. I decided to date for friendship, fun, companionship, and commonality. Nothing serious, nothing sexual, just meeting a variety of men and having a good time. I had no idea how easy this was going to be! I signed up for a thirty-day free trial on Match. com in addition to spending a lot of time out with friends going to fabulous restaurants, lounges, parties, and festivals, traveling for vacations, and attending amazing events, all while surrounding myself with food, art, culture, and music. Within those environments, I was able to meet a variety of men, and they clearly let me know that they were interested in dating me.

It was the *best* dating year of my life. I was almost fifty years old and having a blast on great dates with my choice

of great men. I think my experience was so good because I stayed open, stayed true to who I am, and didn't take it too seriously. I was able to close old doors so that new ones would open. I am very comfortable in my own skin, so when I was ready to date, I was very upfront and honest with everyone about who I was and made sure everyone I met understood that for right now, I was only interested in friendships, meaningful conversation, fun, and common interests—with more than one man.

Yes, ladies, it's OK to date several men at one time. That's why it's called dating! It's not a relationship. It's dating. I gave myself permission to go on as many dates as I wanted to accept and decided to keep my dating age window small. Choosing to date men between the ages of forty-eight and fifty-eight gave me exceptional results. When I tell you that I met some great men who took me on some fantastic and creative dates, please believe me! I had no idea that so many men were still interested in old-school dating and very good

at "courting" a woman like myself. I set my standards high and only went out with men who gave me the vibe that I was looking for. I am so proud of our men out here. Shout out to all the sexy, single, handsome, fun, and respectful gentlemen who treated me like a lady on every date while showing me a fabulous time. You know who you are!

The chief executive officer (CEO), the musician, the pastor, the chef, the technology innovator, the homeland security director, the investment banker, the NYPD officer, the professor, the construction worker, the cardiologist, the chief financial officer (CFO), the entertainment entrepreneur, the accountant, the engineer, the detective, the land developer, the principal, the artist, the professional football player - Go Giants!, the dean of students, the sneaker executive, the firefighter, the physician's assistant, the restaurant owner, and the navy SEAL. All are great men I enjoyed spending time with and had eye-opening

conversations with, and some I have wonderful friendships with to this day.

Dating gave me a freedom that I very much needed. It gave me options and allowed me to decide who I wanted to spend my time with. It also allowed me to see myself and notice things about myself that I either wanted to change or work on to improve. I found that I really liked solid conversations, and the men I connected with the most were the ones who matched me in deep and interesting thought processes. Intelligence is a very attractive quality. I found that I really connected with men who made me think, made me look at things from their perspectives, and allowed me to expand my own views.

I want women to understand that you can have a good time with men who respect you and want to treat you well without having to dilute or change yourself to please them. There are men out there who will love you for exactly who

you are, and they won't feel intimidated by your strong presence and self-assurance. You have to decide what your standards are while accepting people for who they are and where they are at the moment. We teach people how to treat us, so figure out what you want and how you want to be treated while leaving your emotional baggage at the door. Use your self-confidence and open heart as your guide to navigate the wonderful world of dating. I learned so much during the time of meeting new and interesting people and found that dating and connecting can be a joyful and fun experience. It certainly was for me.

# THE "LOVE" PIECE

## UNEXPECTED AND OPEN

*"I am at a point in my life where if it's*
*not incredible, I just don't want it."*

Enters the CFO... all kinds of incredible!

As I am sitting with friends while having a drink at one of my favorite hot spots in King of Prussia, Pennsylvania, I keep catching this man's gaze over and over again. We both smile, we both look away, we both

smile again, and we both look away. Then we smile again, and this time, we don't look away. Rather, we lock eyes.

The only thing I saw was the imaginary halo above his sexy, bald head and his professional demeanor while standing at the other end of the bar with a group of men from his company. I just love a good happy hour!

As my sometimes aggressive Sagittarius self can be, I went over to him, since he was taking too long to come over to me as he was content with flirting a little while longer. Conversation began, and I was stunned at the beautiful accent that flowed out of his mouth. Clearly, he was not from this country. I learned later that he was born and raised in Kenya, East Africa.

We both were interested in getting to know more about each other and decided to meet two days later for drinks.

Drinks turned into appetizers, appetizers turned into dinner, dinner turned into dessert, and dessert turned into six hours later. During this same week, we ended up going on six dates in seven days, and each date lasted over four hours! We simply couldn't get enough of each other and became inseparable. Not only were we inseparable, but we were becoming the best of friends. It was easy and effortless. For this man to make such a profound entrance into my life so unexpectedly, bringing me nothing but peace, joy, acceptance, and friendship, has made me believe that God is delivering me a wonderful blessing that I am so grateful for.

I knew the things that I needed and wanted in order to give my heart and begin a relationship with someone, but I had no idea what I was in for with the international and cultured CFO. This man was making me feel loved, cared for, adored, valuable, special, gorgeous, sexy, feminine, and utterly amazing. He always wants to make me happy and has endless attempts at making me smile. He would listen to

every word that would come out of my mouth and believed that I had something important to offer and say. He saw me and recognized things on the inside that some wouldn't even take the time to see. He was genuinely attentive and passionately affectionate and wanted to be in my presence as much as possible. His behavior and treatment were steady, calming, and most importantly, consistent, always showing me love so complete and in a way that I had never experienced before - nor did I believe was waiting around the corner for me. We are vulnerable with each other and allow our hearts to go deep. We have the same definition of partnership and often share our ideas of lifetime possibilities.

As the CFO and I began to vacation and travel together, he was a wonderful reminder of everything I love and deserve to surround myself in and how wonderful to be able to plan and share international travel with him. We just "get" each other; we naturally mesh; we fit. I like myself in this relationship because he allows me to be true and

authentic, never having to apologize for who I am. When the CFO told me that our only job is to see if we can "out-happy" each other, I knew I had a different kind of man by my side, one who studies my love language in order to please me, knowing that I will do the same for him. We have connected in a way that is rare and special and are both ready and willing to love fully.

Who knows what God has planned for me and the CFO? I will continue to keep my trust in God, knowing that he has put me on this exciting love journey for a reason, a season, or a lifetime, staying open to whatever gifts he has for me to receive.

Wait for the one who simply adores you. The kind of person who brings out the best in you and makes you want to be a better person; the only person who will drop everything to be with you at any time no matter what the circumstances, for the person who makes you smile like no one else ever has. Wait for the person who wants to show you off to the world because they are so proud of you. And most of all, wait for the person who will make you a priority because that's where you belong. (Unknown)

# THE "HAPPILY UNMARRIED" PIECE

## JOY AND FULFILLMENT

The older I get; the more clarity I have on what I desire. As I am a few years post divorced, the one question that seems to keep coming my way is … Would I ever marry again? Although I respect and honor the art of marriage, I can honestly say that I really don't know if I will enter into that kind of merger again. I am sometimes surprised that I would say this because I am such a romantic. I am a lover of love and thrive in relationships. I also have the privilege of being a product of parents who have been married for 54 years. I have seen

it with my own eyes, and I can attest that with hard work, it can be an amazing and fruitful life. Mom and Dad have proven that to me, and I am proud!

Do I believe that you can have passion and purpose with someone and not be married to them? Absolutely! I also believe that happiness doesn't depend on being in a marital relationship nor does it mean that I am not complete unless I am in one. I feel like there should be a warning label within the vows that states - *Marriage could be hazardous to your health, enter at your own risk.* Let me be clear, I believe in the covenant of marriage and its sanctity. I am just not sure it is for me at this moment in my life. Right now, I love my status of being in a serious relationship with my significant other. Have we discussed marriage? Sure, but we have also, more importantly discussed in depth what our ideas of partnership are. What are the visions we have for our lives and do they align with each other's vision? Learning to mesh our aspirations and lifelong possibilities together is

fun and painless when there isn't a looming engagement or marriage mandate above our heads. Going our separate ways after a week or two of sharing the same space allows us to miss and long for each other while at the same time being able to manage our own separate homes in the manner that we each see fit. Coming back together again is exciting and filled with passion beyond belief. Feeling comfortable and confident in letting each other be authentic in who we are is what gives me great joy and fulfillment, and I am thankful that I found someone that meets all my needs.

I was recently complimented on the diamond eternity band that I was wearing and was asked if I was married. I happily answered; no and explained that I metaphorically married myself. I no longer feel the need to conform to the societal norm of reserving my ring-finger for someone else to possibly put a ring on it for me. Not only do I own my fingers, but I also own beautiful rings and lovely pieces of jewelry, and have the choice to display them wherever

I want to on my body; ring-finger included. Marriage is not easy, nor is it the fairytale that little girls read about in nursery rhyme books. He most certainly won't arrive on a white horse and he will most likely save himself before he even thinks of saving the beautiful damsel in distress. The marriage paradigm is so vast and profound that the foundation and function of it in all its variations are difficult to define. The general belief and thought that marriage embodies the highest level of love, sex, intimacy, devotion, fidelity and sacrifice by bringing two people together to become greater than what they once were; is just that; a belief and thought. For me, marriage is no longer the goal. I much rather aim to be fulfilled by allowing my partner and I to stay individuals within our right to live as we see fit for our own personal growth and happiness while sharing a life of joy and discovery.

# THE "WELLNESS" PIECE

## WHOLE FOODS/PLANT-BASED LIFESTYLE

**E**ach year when my birthday rolls around, I find myself grateful and reflective. I also find myself appreciating and striving for wellness. Wellness is the quality or state of being healthy in body and mind. Simple lifestyle changes can dramatically improve our outlook on life and bring abundance and joy to living. I spent many years trying to figure out what works for me, what doesn't work for me, and what will make me feel good on the inside as well as what will wear well on the outside.

Let's be honest: dropping a few pounds is always an added benefit that most of us are seeking. I tried many diets, regimens, and plans and finally realized that as we get older, the same things that might have worked for us in our younger years may not be right for us in our older years. My goals are now more attainable and make sense for a fifty-year-old female body. For me, it comes down to what I fuel my body with and how it physically makes me feel on the inside. I suffer from chronic inflammation so I am always trying to find something that will aid in relieving me from extreme joint, muscle, and nerve pain as well as severe random arthritic flare-ups and migraines.

I did a lot of research and educated myself, learning that nutritional health also equates to physical health. It all comes down to the food that we consume, and quite honestly, I believe that most of what we consume in the standard American diet is poison to our bodies.

My research has led me to adopt a whole foods/plant-based diet, which is an eating pattern that encourages and emphasizes the consumption of natural, unrefined plant foods, such as fruits, vegetables, potatoes, whole grains, beans, nuts, seeds, and limited sugars and discourages and eliminates meat, fish, dairy, eggs, oils, and processed foods.

Taking control of what I choose to put in my body has been a powerful step to boost my energy levels and reduce my risks of illness and inflammation, and it helps to prevent chronic disease. I eliminated fats and junk food from my diet, and my body is now thanking me for it. It's a plan that has allowed me to give up the "diet" label in favor of a "lifestyle." Eating whole foods, rich flavors, and natural ingredients has given me the benefits of a healthy weight and optimum health. I allow food to be thy medicine. I simply just feel better.

Those who know me well know that I love to cook. This lifestyle has allowed me to spend quality time preparing and cooking new recipes using natural, whole ingredients to come up with simple, filling, and delicious meals. This way of eating has satisfied me like no other way I have eaten before. I don't ever have to count points or think about calories. I don't ever have to worry about portion control. I don't ever have to worry about how many meals or snacks I can have each day. I just eat ad libitum, eating as much as I want without any restriction on quantity.

I have even started coaching some friends about the whole foods/plant-based lifestyle, and many have come on board to a new way of eating for themselves and are loving their personal results. When it comes to food and nutrition, it is amazing what you can accomplish simply by changing your thought process as well as your lifestyle.

Let's talk a little bit about fitness. Ugh, exercise and fitness. The two words that give many people anxiety, including me. Based on my own notions about exercise and fitness, I discovered that working out at the gym is just not for me. Been there, done that. It isn't my thing. I tried for years to make it my thing, making sure that I hit the gym three to four times a week, while hating every moment of it. I hated going, and I hated being there. I thought, *Can I keep up with what the person next to me is doing? Is everyone looking at me?* I couldn't stop looking at the clock while walking on the treadmill, wondering if I had done enough to make the visit worth it.

Boy, oh boy, the things we do to ourselves in order to pretend that we are accomplishing something. Ever since I was a little girl, I was extremely athletic, playing on a travel-team softball league for fifteen years, competing on the swim team, roller-skating, riding bikes every weekend, playing volleyball and dodgeball, and always running and playing

outside. I had to remind myself as an adult that I'd much rather be outdoors doing some kind of adventure or activity like hiking, walking, bike riding, or swimming. I'd also rather go dancing and move my body than to be cooped up inside a gym with all my anxious feelings about being there. Just because someone else loves the gym and can't wait to get there each day, doesn't mean that I have to.

I am learning more and more that I have to do *my* thing, and *my* thing may not be someone else's thing. I am happy focusing on what I like and doing what works best for me, always trying to stay authentic in who I am.

# THE "CATHARTIC" PIECES

## JOURNALING, MEDITATION, PRAYER

When it comes to finding my center and balance within, this is where it all begins for me. For as long as I can remember, I was always drawn to writing. Not necessarily typing on a computer or laptop but good, old-fashioned, pen-to-paper kind of writing. Letter writing, writing lists, note-taking, scheduling, and most importantly and most rewarding, writing in a journal.

I never really understood why writing felt so good to me until I was in my college years and realized it gave me a peace of mind and a safe place to let out all of my feelings and emotions without worrying about judgment or feedback. When it comes to finding balance, peace, and contentment, writing has always been my outlet. There is something about quietly sitting down with my many thoughts, questions, desires, and dreams and expressing them on paper. I often wondered why it felt so good—why putting pen to paper was so satisfying and gave me such pleasure. I enjoyed the many times I would go back to read some of the things I was so passionate about at random moments in my life and how, in all my years of journaling, there seemed to be one consistent thread: how I was changing and evolving and always had a mindset of growth and a desire to be better than I was at the moment. I was always wondering and having a feeling of greatness and the pursuit of my authenticity and purpose.

I later learned that my journal writing formed a collection of stories that I would one day organize and turn into a book or some kind of template to hopefully help someone else.

Journaling makes me feel comforted. It makes me feel warm and whole. I trust it. I trust what I say, I trust what I put on paper, and I trust that the words are mine and nobody else can claim, diminish, or turn them into something that they are not. It feels really good to be in charge of my own thoughts and put those words into some form of action simply by placing them in a journal.

Journaling can give you a road map and ideas so that you can use those words later to form the life that you want for yourself. I learned that my words were special and powerful and that they were a literary energy that only I could tap into. I didn't have to express it or explain it to anybody else. I love that it was my journal and they were just my words.

Another form of peace and contentment for me is the art of meditation. Meditation is the complete opposite of journal writing. Meditation doesn't use words at all but uses thoughts and energies by focusing on your breath to give you balance, mindfulness, and awareness. It is a practice to increase calmness and physical relaxation. Being able to quiet your mind and put yourself in a place of peace and quiet concentration. Meditation is a time for me to connect the mental dots, to sit or lay in my stillness and honor and reverence God. It's a time for mindful purging. A time to search for inner peace and balance, while trying to quiet the negative and looping thoughts that are always trying to enter.

I call meditation my mind-body medicine. I allow myself to drift off into a blissful, safe haven, which is always surrounded by calm waters, with the fragrance of the sea that I am actually sometimes able to smell. Here is where I find warmth, clarity, and calm. Meditation always leads me into prayer, which is simply intimate conversations with God.

It's the time to ask, time to confess, time to confer, time to listen, and time to simply say thank-you for all that he has done and continues to do in my life. Through prayer, I find strength and can feel the presence of God. I have the honor of falling before his throne every day, several times a day.

I truly believe in the power of prayer and without a doubt believe that prayer changes things. Prayer is consistent with faith. Praying while at the same time having faith in whatever decision God makes. Trying not to question when things don't go the way I may want them to and learning to trust that God is in control and knows what's best for me and my life. Through prayer, I am reminded that there is indeed a supreme being, the all-powerful, all-knowing, all-present, eternal existence of the Creator I call God. He is my counselor, comforter, and healer. He is my light in darkness,

he is the source of my strength, he is the center of my life, and all things come from him.

My personal passage that securely keeps my life balanced and grounded starts and ends with journaling, meditating, and praying, and for that, I am forever grateful.

# THE "NEXT" PIECE

## LIFE COACHING PURPOSE

C ounseling is professional guidance in resolving personal and social problems and difficulties, centered in mental health and wellness. Life coaching is supporting and partnering with clients in a thought-provoking and creative process that inspires them to maximize their personal and professional potential; it is help with filling in the gaps of our master plan and clarifying the path from where we are to where we want to be.

While on this life journey, I have learned many lessons—hard ones and easy ones. I have lived to experience many things, both positive and negative. Some shared and some sacredly kept inside. As I ease into the next phase of my life, I often ask myself, "What is my purpose? Where is my power base? What's next for me? How can I fulfill the highest, truest expression of myself? What's deep in my soul that needs to get out? Where can I be of good service? What's God's plan for me, and how can I help another?"

Sometimes the very thing that you have been doing in a casual way is the very thing that you are supposed to be doing in a more formal and structured way. I have always had a passion for self-development and personal growth and have always been the person friends and family come to for advice, my perspective, my input, and my trust. I was once told that I seem to move through life with confidence and joy, and although I believe that is just who I am, I also think that it is something that can be acquired.

I naturally gravitated toward being a certified professional life coach because I have a special skill set with a unique ability, natural passion, and desire to empower and inspire others. I love and enjoy thought-provoking conversations and strive to make every effort to motivate and challenge women and men to achieve their goals by helping them tap into their full potential and discover their true authentic self. Once these concepts are learned, we have the ability to move life forward.

I find that I am able to help create a space that focuses on personal growth and happiness, and I am able to provide constructive feedback, which can help people move toward the life they desire. We are all born with unique talents; it is important to me to be the bridge to help bring those amazing qualities into alignment for a strong sense of purpose and direction to everyday life.

I believe that through many authentic conversations, it will become clear how powerful, capable, and resourceful we all are, learning to trust in ourselves along the way and listen to ourselves more deeply. By having courageous conversations, we are able to recognize our own limiting beliefs so that we can move toward the life we really want and feel encouraged to build our own self-esteem. Sometimes being able to clearly articulate our own values and dreams enables us to make more meaningful choices with consistent action. I want women and men to recognize that self-care should be at the top of their to-do list and that it is up to them to choose the direction they want to go—and take responsibility for that direction.

Transformation is a real journey, and it can power our lives forward. I get so much joy and fulfilment working with amazing people who trust me to help them fill in the gaps and assist them in doing the work that is involved with feeling whole, complete, and satisfied. Every living being

goes through difficult and trying times. Life is known to throw us through some unimaginable loops and hurdles. We all have broken pieces and shards of life that, no matter how hard we may have tried, we just couldn't keep them together. Paying attention to what is already inside us, reaching down deep to whatever it is that we are yearning for, and pulling it out so that we can rescue our own lives is crucial.

The feelings of worth and fulfillment bring about a self-love that can sometimes be indescribable. It can literally be the tools that you need to propel your life forward, live in your true authenticity and create a life that you love.

**Stephanie C. Smalls** is a certified professional life coach who is deeply interested in personal growth and self-development. Her core competencies include a depth of emotional intelligence, learning agility, innate curiosity, respect for differences, and a willingness to be in service to others. She is self-motivated to contribute her best to whatever she pursues. With the gift of good insight into people and situations, she is a natural coach. As evidence of that fact, many people in her professional and personal life turn to her for a listening ear, to benefit from the provocative questions she asks, and to help them sort through and detangle complex challenges. Authentic, respectful, patient and present, people readily trust Stephanie. That trust creates space for candid, open dialogue, which is the quality of communication that supports clients in achieving life-changing breakthroughs. She specializes in authenticity and fulfillment, women's empowerment, self-love and discovery, dating after divorce, mindset awareness, and growth goals. Visit her online at www.smallscoaching.com.

Stephanie C. Smalls

Certified Professional Life Coach

Specializing in:

- Authenticity & Fulfillment
- Women's Empowerment
- Self-Love & Discovery
- Dating after Divorce
- Mindset Awareness
- Growth Goals

Email: Steph@SmallsCoaching.com

Website: www.SmallsCoaching.com

Printed in the United States
by Baker & Taylor Publisher Services